Mel Bay's

Basic Recorder Method

By
Dr. William M. Weiss

MEL BAY

1 2 3 4 5 6 7 8 9 0

© 1981 BY MEL BAY PUBLICATIONS INC., PACIFIC, MO.
INTERNATIONAL COPYRIGHT SECURED. ALL RIGHTS RESERVED. PRINTED IN U.S.A.

FOREWORD

The recorder should be studied and played in the same manner as any other musical instrument. Students, whether in elementary, middle or secondary schools, or in college methods courses, as well as adult beginners, should learn to play the recorder in a systematic, sequential manner. It is important for the student to develop the necessary technical and mechanical skills from the very beginning in order to produce lovely sound and to play with rhythmic accuracy.

This method will help develop the necessary skills by introducing through a rote to note method, correct blowing, tonguing and fingering technics. The basic rudiments of music will be introduced at appropriate places in the text.

Material based on folk songs from around the world will be introduced early in a sequential manner to heighten and to maintain the interest of the student in the progress towards mastery of the instrument.

The uniqueness of this recorder instrumental method is the manner in which elements of the Suzuki and Kodaly systems of music education have been adapted and incorporated into a creative design of instruction. "Rote to Note" is the basic approach. The recorder player should be able to produce good sound and have control over the various finger positions before attempting to read the notation. A gradual and systematic introduction of note reading will encourage the student to continue playing without the frustration of having to cope with musical notation at an early stage.

With Mel Bay's "Basic Recorder Method," the student, whether alone or in a group or class, should be able to progress easily and successfully and to play the vast amount of beautiful solo and ensemble recorder music.

ABOUT THE AUTHOR

The "Basic Recorder Method" has been written by Dr. William M. Weiss, Director of Music Education, Public Schools Newark, New Jersey.

In addition to his position with the Newark Public Schools, Dr. Weiss has engaged in a number of other musical and professional activities. Among them are the following: member of the New Jersey Symphony Orchestra; conductor of the Newark Symphony Orchestra; member of the American Recorder Society; Adjunct Instructor in Music Education at Rutgers University; Douglas College, Kean State College; Board of Directors, New Jersey Music Educators Association; Board of Examiners, New York City Board of Education.

This method has been used extensively by Dr. Weiss in various situations. It has proven to be successful both from the standpoint of student appeal and as a means of developing musical learning.

CONTENTS

The Recorder	4
The Care of the Recorder	4
Instructions for Holding and Playing the Recorder	5
Fingering	6
Marching Song	9
A Duet	10
A Children's Song	10
A Dance Waltz	11
Dance a Waltz	11
Duke of York	12
Go From My Window	12
Dance	12
Jingle Bells	14
Who's That Tapping at the Window	14
Hello Girls	14
Cuckoo Song	15
Zoom, Zoom, Zoom	15
Merrily We Roll Along	15
Playground Song	15
J'ai Du Bon Babac (I Have Some Good Tobacco)	16
Go Tell Aunt Rhody	16
Lightly Row	16
Lover's Lament	18
A Dance	18
Mountain Song	19
Short'ning Bread	19
Dinah	19
Neopolitan Dance	21
Polka	21
Swinging Along	22
Old Chisolm Trail	22
Crescent Moon	24
Folk Tune	24
Dreams	25
Hush Little Baby	25
A Sad Dance	25
Etude I—C Scale	27
Etude II	27
Etude III	27
Amaryllis	28
The Moon is Coming Out	28
Billy Boy	28
Hatikvah—National Anthem	29
Where Do You Go	30
This Old Man	30
Sweetly Sings the Donkey	30
Animal Farm Song	31
Ode to Joy—9th Symphony	31
A Song with F Sharp	32
La Vibora—The Sea Serpent	32
Aura Lee	33
Tatra Mountain	33
America	34
Bingo	34
Red River Valley	34
Annie Laurie	35
Mary Had a Baby	36
Sailing on the Ocean	36
Steal, Away	36
A Folk Ballad	37
The Garden	37
All Night, All Day	37
Auld Lang Syne	38
Drink to Me Only	39
Tum Balalaika	40
Early One Morning	40
On Top of Old Smoky	41
Kookaburra	41
Chanukah	41
Study	42
Silent Night	42
The Bridge of Avignon	44
Marines' Hymn	44
Hurry Good Shepherds	45
Etude	46
Sweet Betsy from Pike	47
Give Us Permission	47
Piñata Song	48
Alleluia	48
The Night is Serene	49
Bye 'M Bye	49
Prayer of Thanksgiving	50
Shepherds Came to Bethlehem—Carol	50
Etude in B Flat	51
Circle Around	52
Music Alone Shall Live	52
She Watched Her Sheep	53
A Folk Tune	53
One More River	54
Folk Song	54
Fingering Chart—Soprano Recorder	55

THE RECORDER

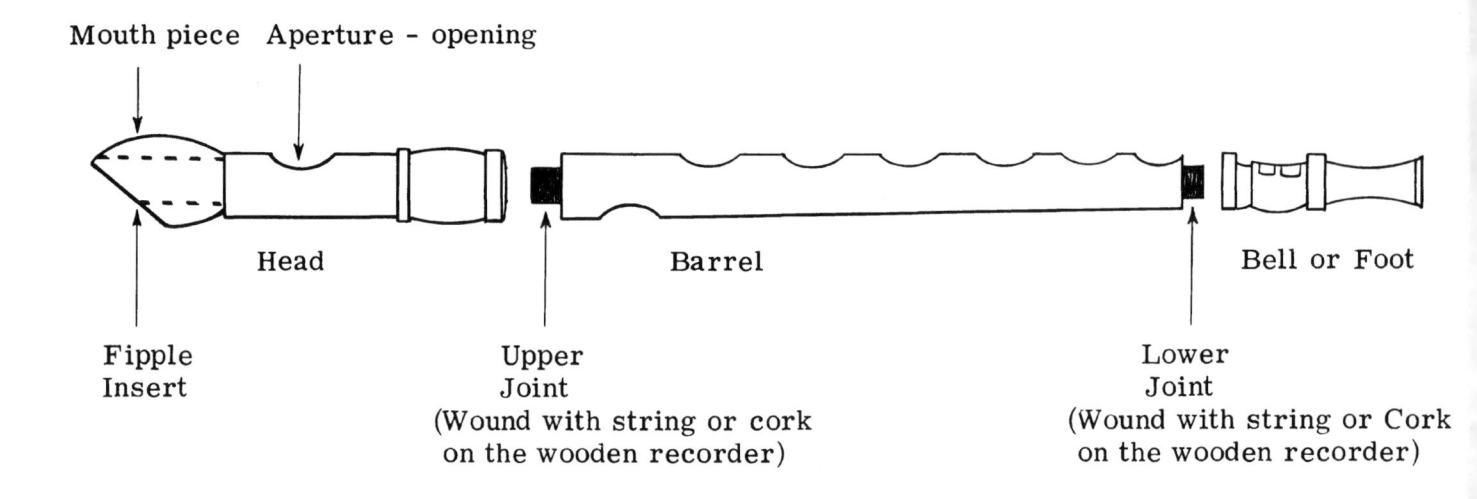

Mouth piece   Aperture - opening

Head   Barrel   Bell or Foot

Fipple Insert

Upper Joint
(Wound with string or cork on the wooden recorder)

Lower Joint
(Wound with string or Cork on the wooden recorder)

THE CARE OF THE RECORDER

The author recommends the use of a plastic recorder for the beginning player. There are a number of well-made and "in-tune" plastic recorders of excellent quality. They require less care and attention than wooden recorders. When a student has reached a fairly high level of performance then he or she might change over to a good wooden one.

Plastic recorders should be cleaned frequently by running luke-warm water through the instrument. It will be necessary to shake the water thoroughly from the recorder after it is cleaned. The mouth piece should be washed with a mild soap and luke-warm water occasionally.

Wooden recorders should be held in the hands or under the arm for a short time in order to "warm-up" the instrument. After playing, the recorder should be dried with a swab or chamois.

New wooden recorders should be played for short periods of time- fifteen to twenty minutes at the beginning. Wooden recorders should not be exposed to extreme changes of temperatures.

Cork grease should be applied to joints regularly if the fit is tight.

INSTRUCTIONS FOR HOLDING AND PLAYING THE RECORDER

Hold the recorder with the *left first finger covering the top hole and the left thumb covering the hole in the back.*

The right thumb supports the recorder by placing it about 3 to 4 inches below the left thumb. *There is no hole to cover by the right hand thumb.*

Place the mouthpiece between the lips but do not allow the teeth to touch the mouthpiece. No more than one-half inch of the mouthpiece should be placed between the lips. Do not bite or press the lips too hard against the mouthpiece. Blow softly and easily into the mouthpiece with a soft *ta* or *tee* sound. Loud or strong blowing will cause the recorder to respond with a high squeeking or shrieking sound.

Make sure that the top hole and the hole in the back of the recorder are covered completely by the pads of the left first finger and the left thumb.

The recorder should be held at a forty-five degree angle with the arms hanging loosely and slightly away from the body.

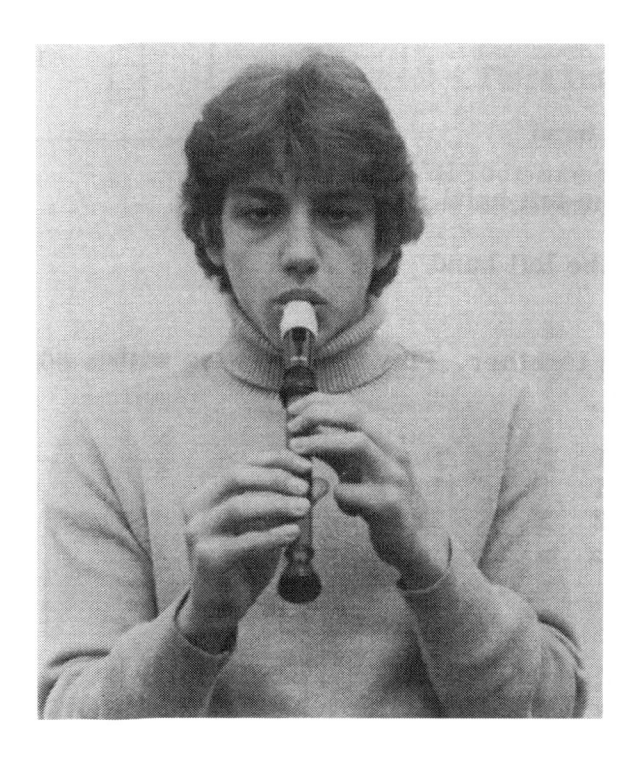

DUKE OF YORK

Lively　　　　　　　　　　　　　　　　　　　　　　　　　　　　　　England

○ Whole note - 4 Counts

𝅗𝅥. Dotted halfnote - 3 counts

GO FROM MY WINDOW

Evenly　　　　　　　　　　　　　　　　　　　　　　　　　Old English Song

DANCE

Lively　　　　　　　　　　　　　　　　　　　　　　　　　　　　　Holland

This note is called D. It is on the third line from the bottom. D is played with the second finger of the left hand alone. Remove the left thumb. Support the recorder with the right thumb.

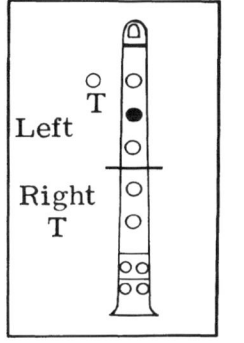

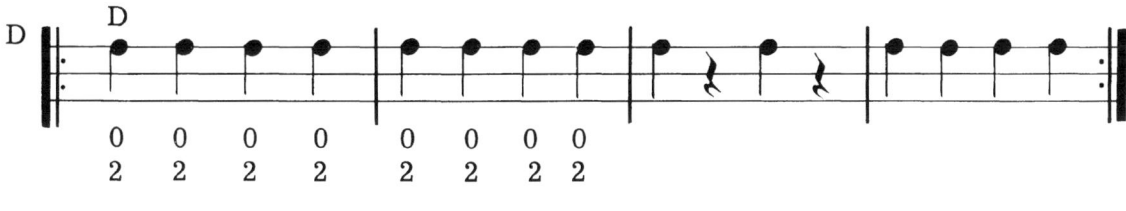

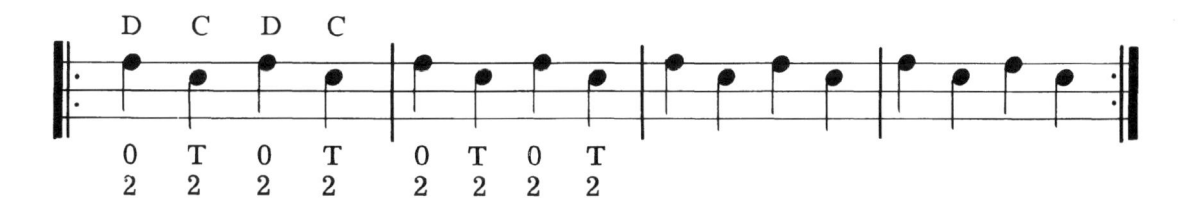

Left / Right

D | D
0 0 0 0 | 0 0 0 0
2 2 2 2 | 2 2 2 2

D C D C
0 T 0 T | 0 T 0 T
2 2 2 2 | 2 2 2 2

From D to C simply add your left thumb

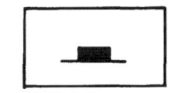

D C B C
0 T T T
2 2 1 2

Half rest - 2 counts

D C B A
0 T T T
2 2 1 1
    2

D C B A G
0 T T T T
2 2 1 1 1
    2 2
      3

D B G B

LOVER'S LAMENT

Slowly — Orient

A DANCE

Swing along — Sweden

MOUNTAIN SONG

America

SHORT'NING BREAD

Southern American

DINAH

America

This note is called E. It is located on the bottom line. It is played with the first three fingers and thumb of the left hand and the first two fingers of the right hand.

E

L T
  1
  2
  3
R 1
T 2

E F E F

  T T T T
L 1 1 1 1
  2 2 2 2
  3 3 3 3
R 1 1 1 1
T 2 3 2 3

| From E to F in the Baroque simply exchange the third finger on the right hand for the second. | In the German raise the second finger going from E to F |

E F G F

NEOPOLITAN DANCE

Lively — Italy

POLKA

Lively — Poland

SWINGING ALONG

Livey
America

OLD CHISOLM TRAIL

Slowly
America

It is now time to add the top or final line to the music staff. There are five lines upon which music is placed. The lines are: <u>E</u> <u>G</u> <u>B</u> <u>D</u> <u>F</u>. E is the lowest and F the highest.

This is called the <u>G clef.</u> It is placed on the <u>treble staff</u> of five lines and circles the second line to tell where G is placed.

This note is called <u>D</u>. It is placed on the space below the bottom or first line. It is played with the three fingers and thumb of the left hand and the three fingers of the right hand.

Be sure to cover the two small holes with the third finger of the right hand.

When playing from D to E simply raise the third finger of the right hand and then return it to play E to D

CRESCENT MOON

China

Unhurried

FOLK TUNE

Moravia

Lively

DREAMS

HUSH LITTLE BABY

A SAD DANCE

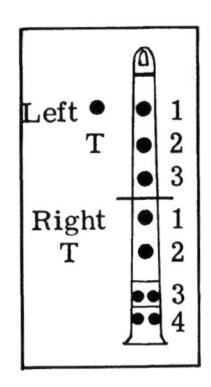

The lowest tone or note on the recorder is C. It is placed on an added line below the staff.

Make sure that the third and fourth fingers of the right hand cover the small double holes.

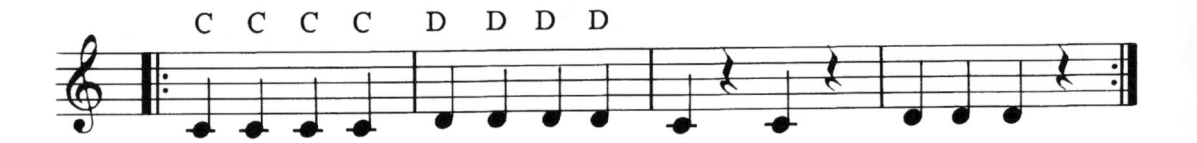

When playing C to D simply raise the fourth finger.
When playing from D to C return the fourth finger.

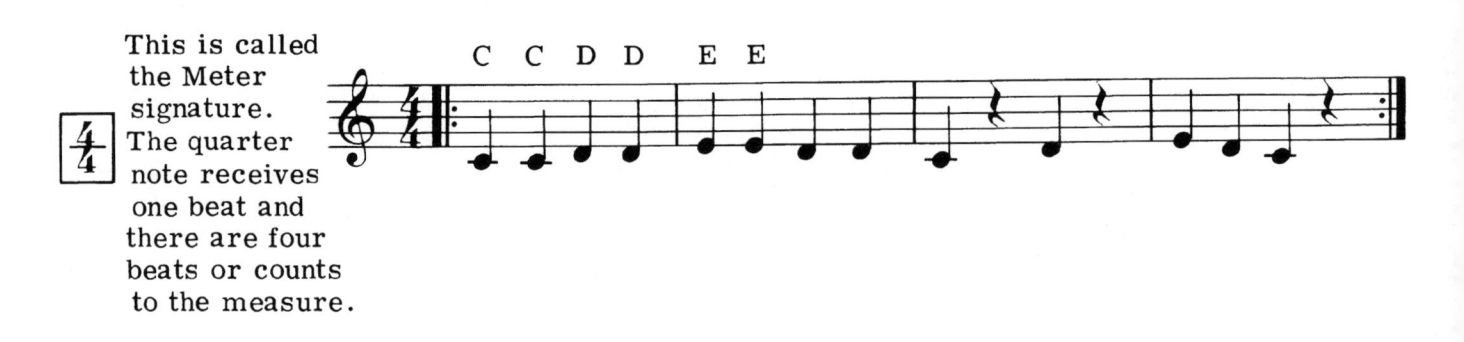

This is called the Meter signature. **4/4** The quarter note receives one beat and there are four beats or counts to the measure.

26

ETUDE I-C SCALE

Etude — A musical study

ETUDE II

$\boxed{\dfrac{3}{4}}$ 3 counts to the measure. The quarter note receives one count.

ETUDE III

Key of C — There are no sharps or flats in the signature

AMARYLLIS
France
Evenly

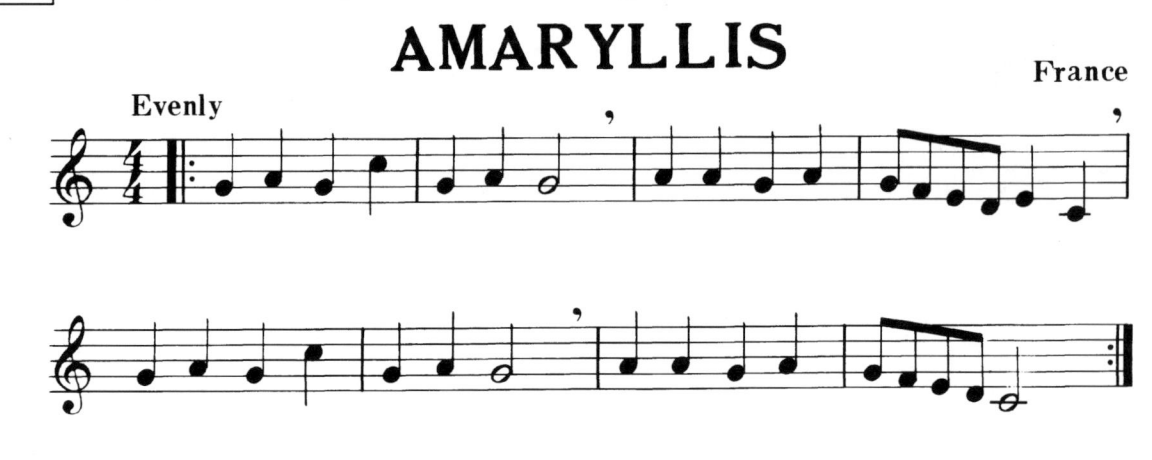

THE MOON IS COMING OUT
Japan
Serenely

2/4 — Two counts to the measure. The quarter note receives one count.

BILLY BOY
America
Lively

Tie — The tie is a curved line connecting two notes of the same pitch. The notes are played and counted as one note.

♭ flat   The flat lowers the note one-half step or tone.

This note is called <u>B flat.</u> It is on the third or middle line and it is one-half step or one half tone lower than B. It is played by the first and third fingers and thumb of the left hand and the first and third fingers of the right hand. When a flat appears on the third line all Bs are flat.

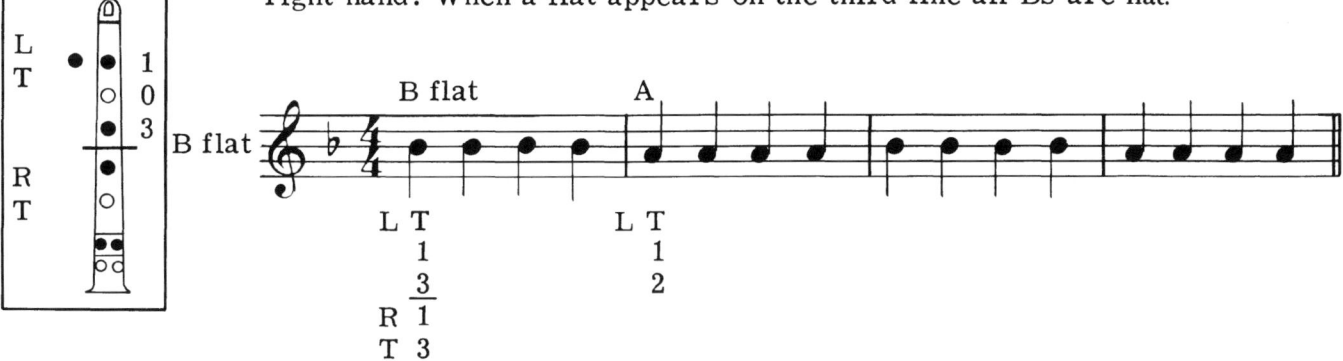

Key of F Major   The flat (♭) is placed on the third line. The B on the third line now becomes B flat. When there is one flat on the staff - B flat - the key is called F Major.

HATIKVAH-NATIONAL ANTHEM

Israel

Slowly

B flat

WHERE DO YOU GO

Evenly　　　　　　　　　　　　　　　　　　　　　　　　　　　　French-Canadian

THIS OLD MAN

American Children's Song

Fast

SWEETLY SINGS THE DONKEY

Moderately　　　　　　　　　　　　　　　　　　　　　　　　　American

ANIMAL FARM SONG

Israel

Lively

ODE TO JOY - 9TH SYMPHONY

Beethoven

Brightly

long short long short long short long short 1 2 and 3 4
1   2 and 1   2 and
The dot replaces the eighth note

Sharp

The sharp raises a note one-half step or tone.

This note is called F sharp. It is on the first space. It is one half step or tone above F. It is played by the first, second, third fingers and thumb of the left hand and the second and third fingers of the right hand.

When a sharp appears on the top line all Fs are sharp.
When there is one sharp on the staff - the key is call G major.

A SONG WITH F SHARP

WMW

Key of G Major

LA VIBORA-THE SEA SERPENT

Lively   Spain

32

AURA LEE

Quietly
America

TATRA MOUNTAIN

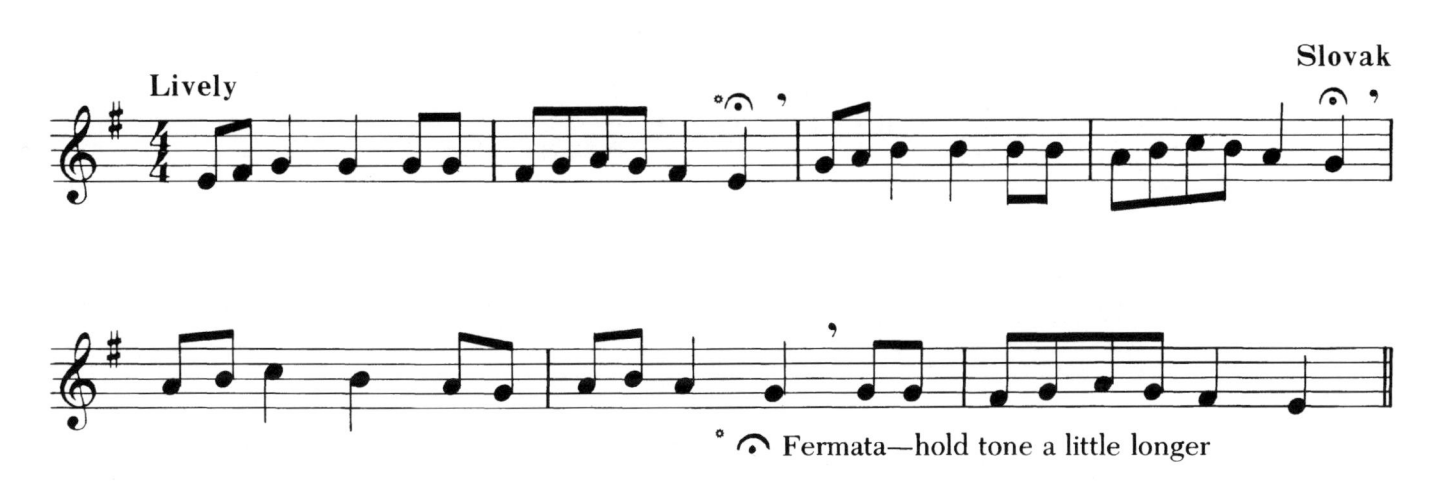

Lively
Slovak

° 𝄐 Fermata—hold tone a little longer

AMERICA

Moderate

°See page 35

BINGO

American

Lively

RED RIVER VALLEY

American

Smoothly

The high notes are played with the left thumb hole partially uncovered. Simply bend the thumb. Do not remove the thumb. This note is high E. It is played with the left first, second and third fingers, the first and second fingers of the right hand and the left thumb bending, partially uncovering the thumb hole. This is called "pinching the hole".

High E

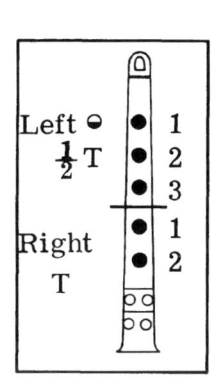

ANNIE LAURIE

Ireland

Smoothly

MARY HAD A BABY

Unhurried — Spiritual

SAILING ON THE OCEAN

Lively — American Game

STEAL, AWAY

Slowly-Quietly — Spiritual

A FOLK BALLAD

Lively — America

THE GARDEN

Smoothly — China

ALL NIGHT, ALL DAY

Evenly — Spiritual

This note is called high **F**. It is on the top line and it is played with the first, second, third fingers of the left hand, the first and third fingers of the right hand with the left thumb hole half covered.

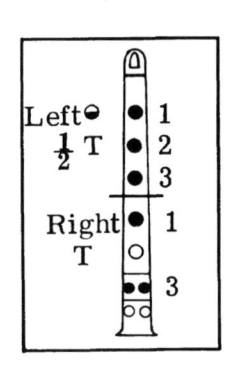

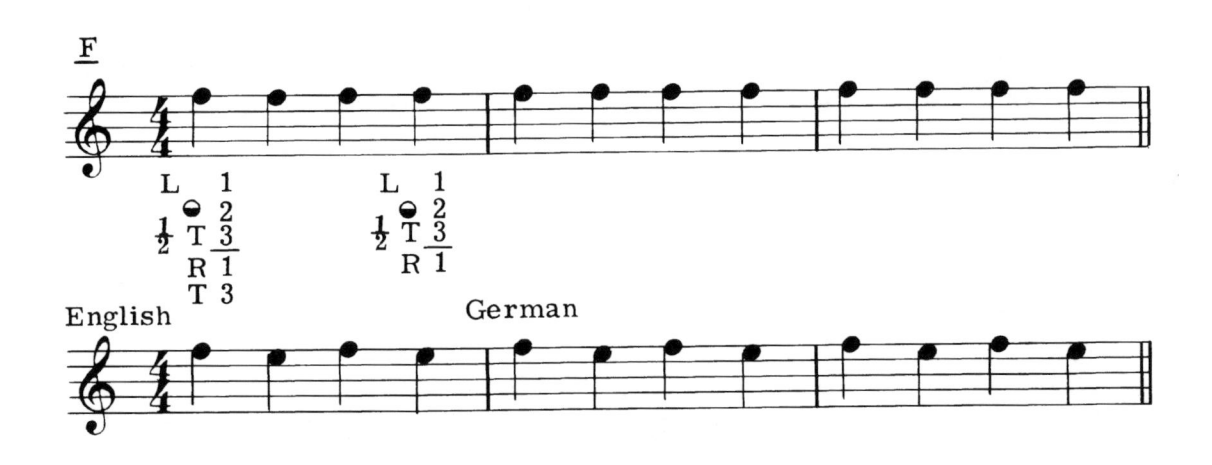

AULD LANG SYNE

Scotland

F Major Scale - Key of F
In the Key of F the note B is played B flat.

Six counts to the measure. The eighth note receives the beat or count. The quarter note receives 2 counts.

DRINK TO ME ONLY

England

Quietly

TUM BALALAIKA

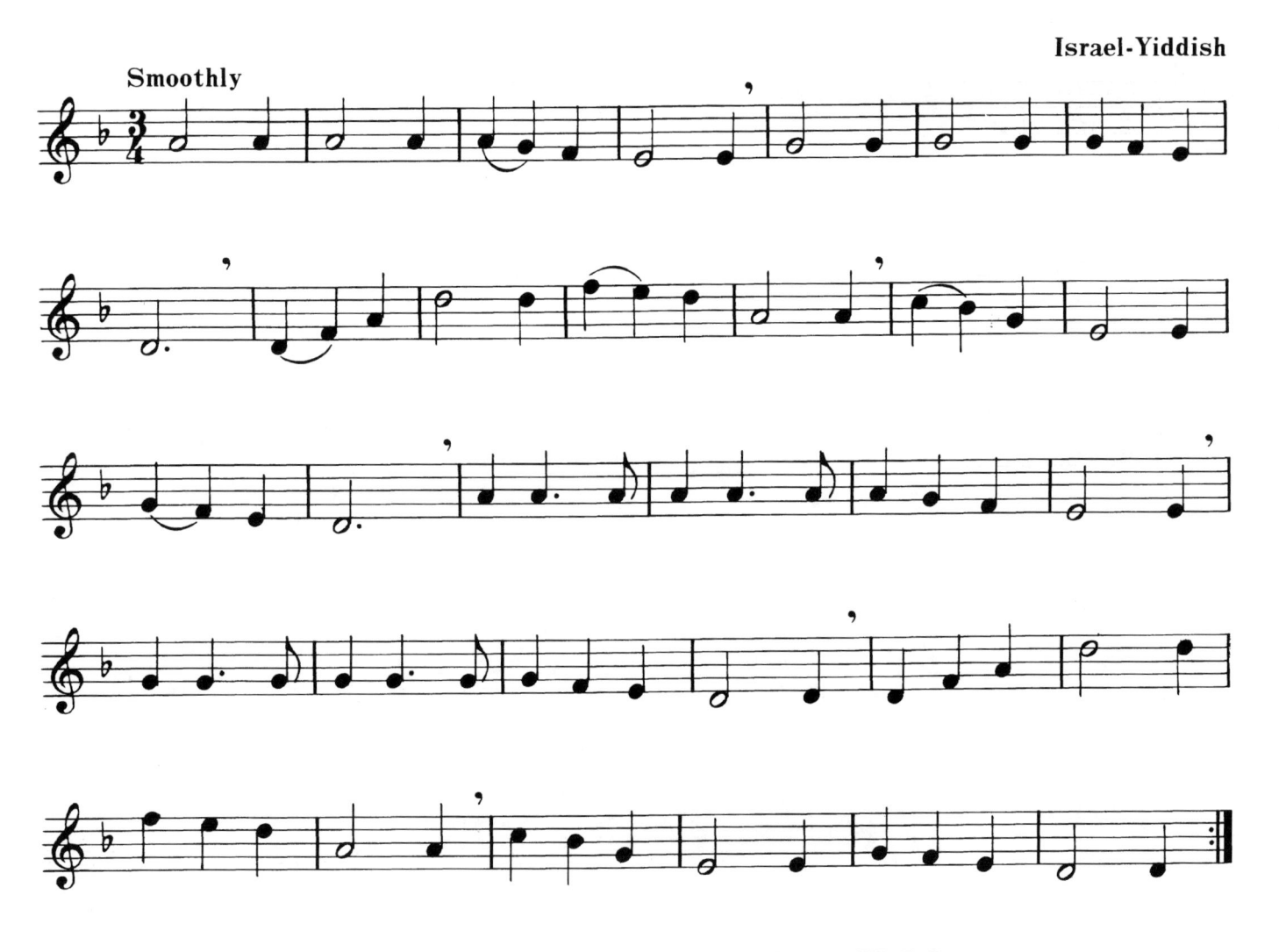

Israel-Yiddish

ON TOP OF OLD SMOKY

America

Unhurried

KOOKABURRA

Australia

Lively

CHANUKAH

Israel

Joyfully

Dotted eighth and sixteenth note rhythm

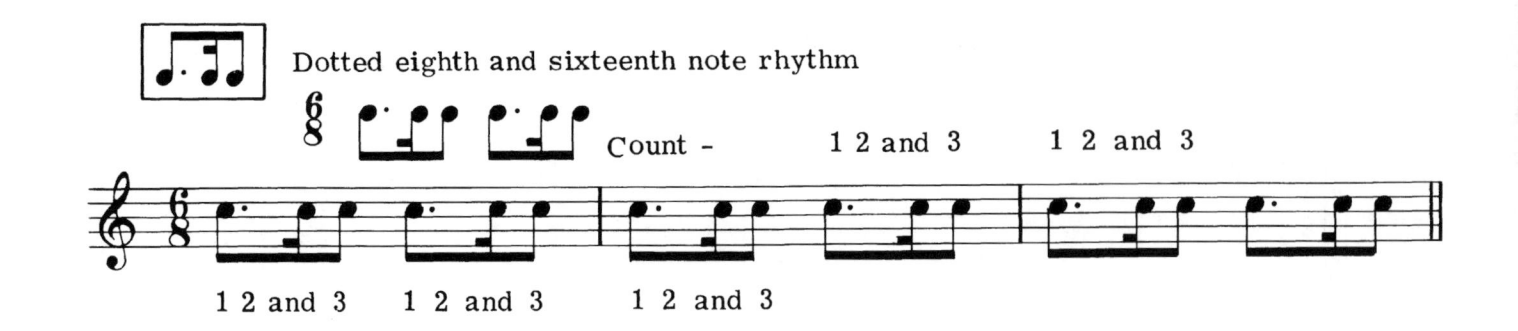

Count -   1 2 and 3   1 2 and 3

1 2 and 3   1 2 and 3   1 2 and 3

STUDY

SILENT NIGHT

F. Gruber

Quietly

This note is called high F sharp. It is on the top line and it is played by the left first, second, third fingers and the right second finger with the left hole half covered.

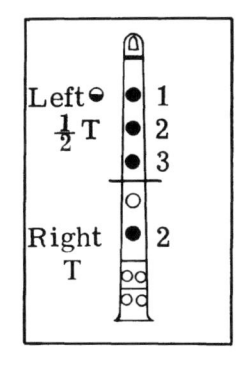

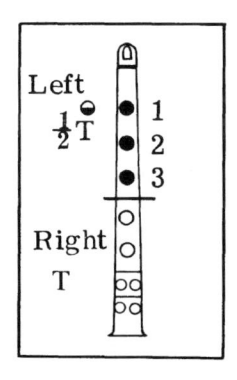

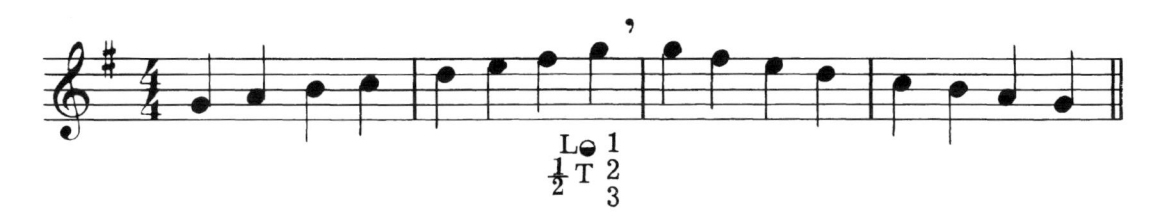

This note is G. It is placed on the top of the fifth line. It is played by the left first, second and third fingers and with the left hole half covered.

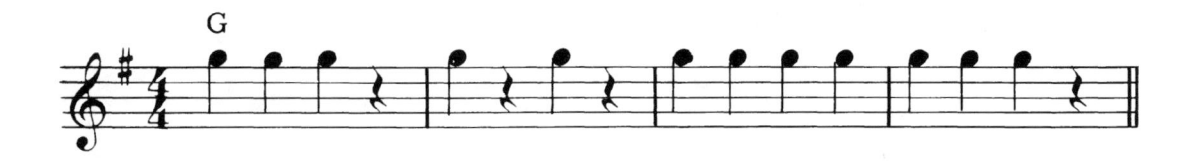

When a sharp is placed on F the top line, both the low F on the first space and the F on the top line are played F sharp.

Key of G

F sharp

G chord

THE BRIDGE OF AVIGNON

France

Gaily

MARINES' HYMN

Marine Corps

Brightly

HURRY, GOOD SHEPHERDS

Puerto Rico

This note is called C sharp. It is played with the left first and second fingers without the left thumb.

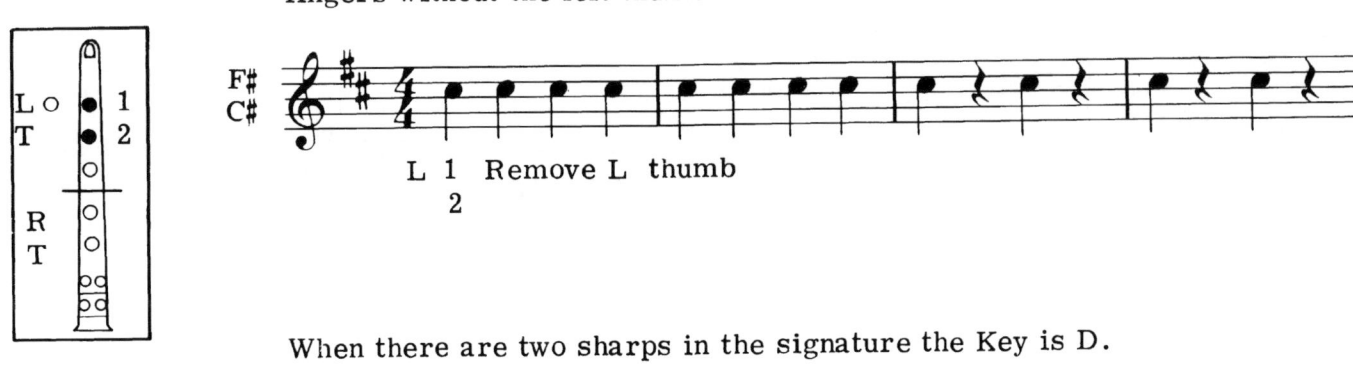

L 1   Remove L thumb
 2

When there are two sharps in the signature the Key is D.

Key of D Major

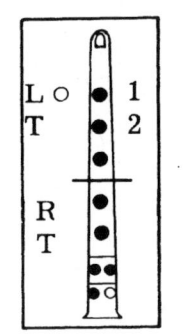

Low C sharp. Right fourth finger covers only one hole.

ETUDE

SWEET BETSY FROM PIKE

Western

Lightly

GIVE US PERMISSION

Brazil

Moderate

PIÑATA SONG

Mexico

Gaily

C sharp

C Natural

ALLELUIA

J. Haydn

Quietly

C Sharp

C Sharp

THE NIGHT IS SERENE

Peacefully　　　　　　　　　　　　　　　　　　　　　　　　Spain

BYE'M BYE

Slowly　　　　　　　　　　　　　　　　　　Texas Folk Song

PRAYER OF THANKSGIVING

Netherlands

Quietly

SHEPHERDS CAME TO BETHLEHEM-CAROL

Poland

Slowly

C sharp

Key of B flat

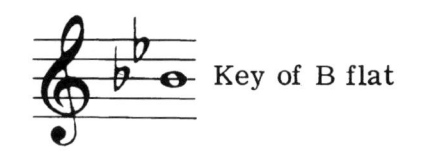

High E flat is played with the second and third fingers of the left hand with the left thumb off and with the first, second and third fingers of the right hand. Low E flat is played with left first, second and third fingers plus thumb and the right first and second fingers. The third finger covers half of the two holes. When there are two flats in the signature the key is called B flat.

High E flat

Low E flat

E flat

E flat

ETUDE IN B FLAT

E flat   E flat

E flat

CIRCLE AROUND

Germany

MUSIC ALONE SHALL LIVE

Germany

SHE WATCHED HER SHEEP

France

Quietly

A FOLK TUNE

Belgium

Briskly

ONE MORE RIVER

Spiritual

Brightly

FOLK SONG

South Africa

Moderate

FINGERING CHART
SOPRANO RECORDER

L - Left   R - Right
T - Thumb   T - Thumb

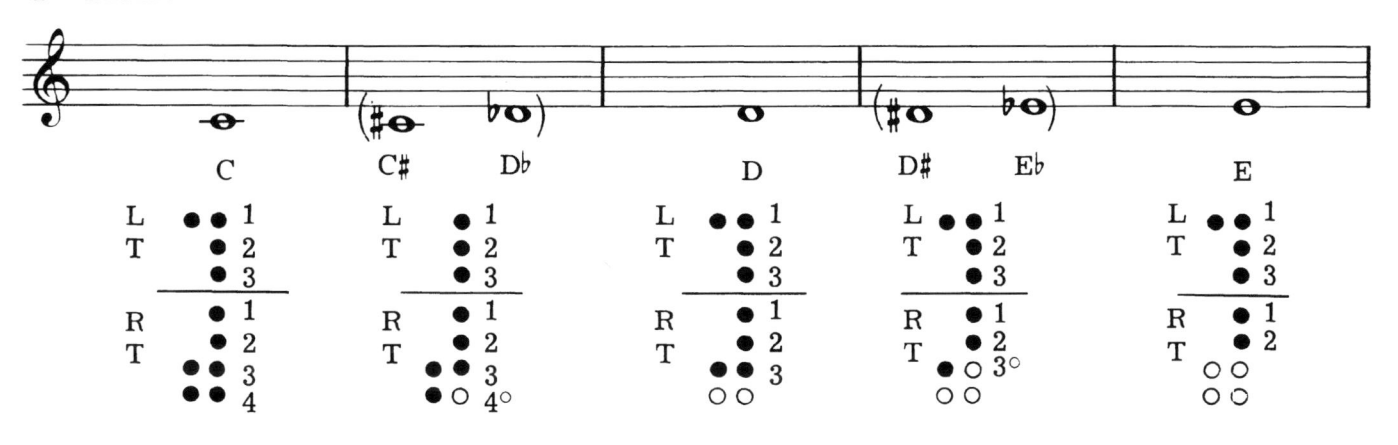

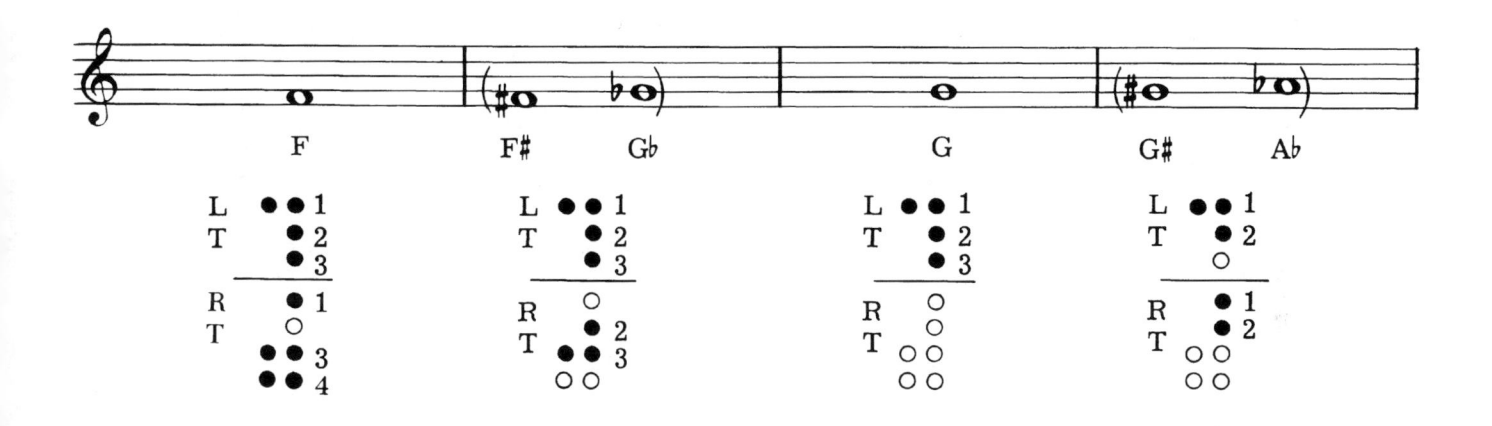

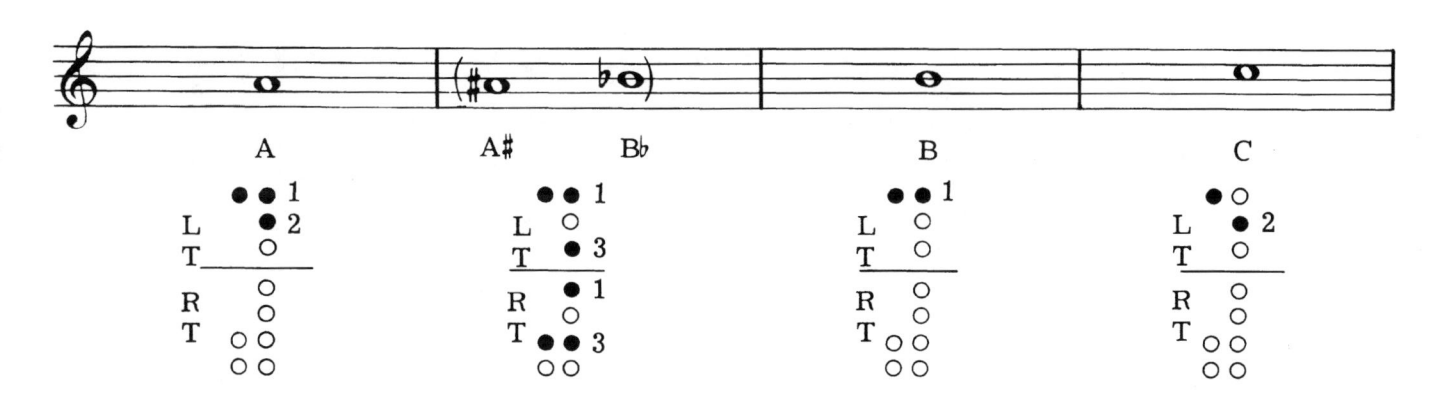

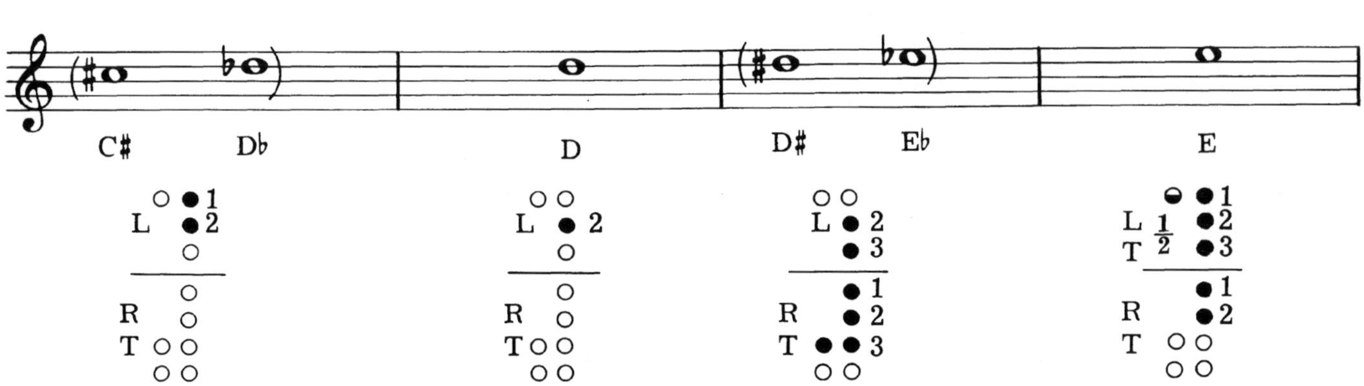
C♯
D♭
D
D♯
E♭
E

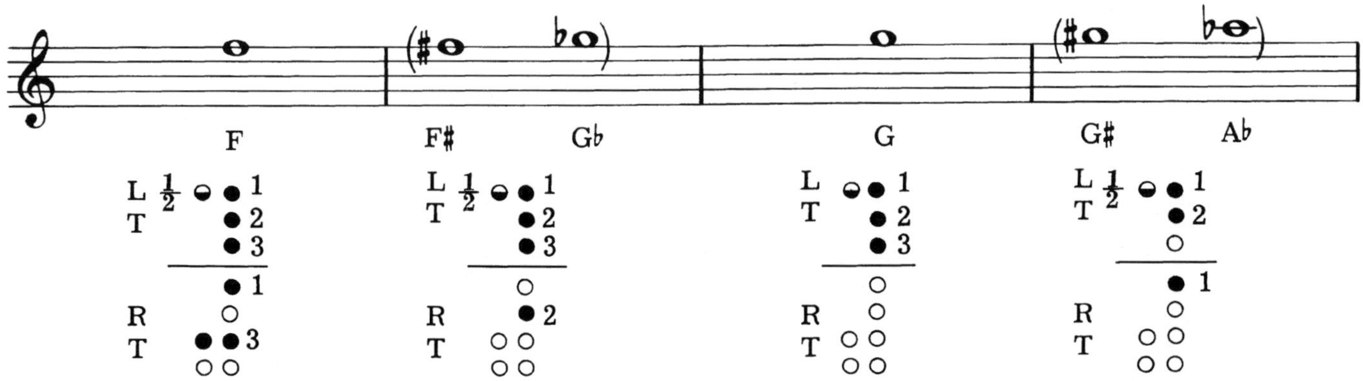
F
F♯
G♭
G
G♯
A♭

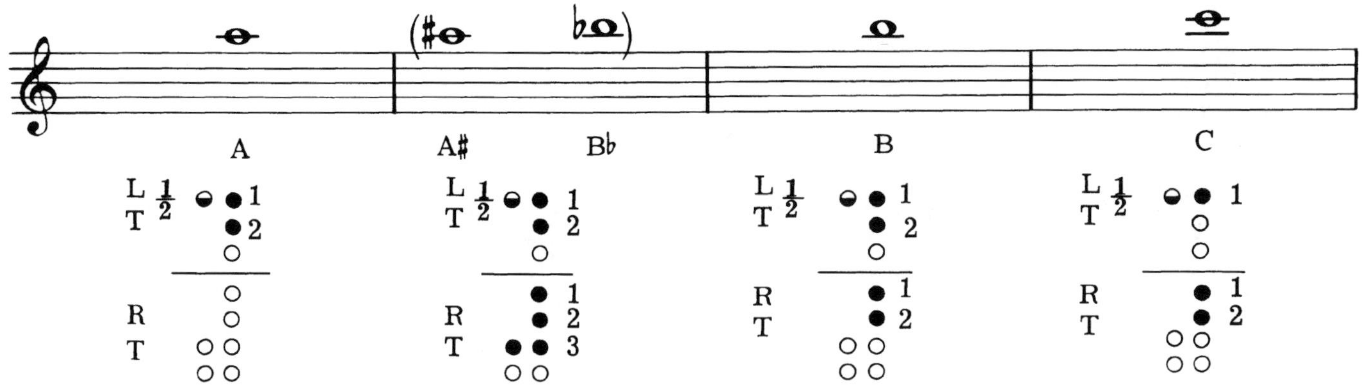
A
A♯
B♭
B
C

Made in the USA
San Bernardino, CA
19 November 2016